LIFE RULES
STUDY GUIDE

LIFE RULES

STUDY GUIDE

ANDY STANLEY

Multnomah Books

LIFE RULES STUDY GUIDE
published by Multnomah Books
A division of Random House, Inc.

International Standard Book Number: 978-1-59052-493-0

Printed in the United States of America

For information:
MULTNOMAH BOOKS
12265 ORACLE BOULEVARD, SUITE 200
COLORADO SPRINGS, CO 80921

08 09 10 — 10 9

Contents

Unwritten Rules

by Andy Stanley

Every set of relationships in life has a corresponding set of rules. These life rules are usually unspoken. And they're certainly unwritten. But whether you find yourself among family, in the office, or with friends, there are distinct rules that apply.

For example, at work or in school the rule may be, "Every man for himself" or, "Do unto others as they've done unto you." With friends, it may be, "You look out for me and I'll look out for you" or, "An eye for an eye." In your family, it could be, "Blood runs thicker than water" or, "Don't mess with me and I won't mess with you." Keep in mind, most of these rules are at work under the surface. We don't talk about them, we don't think about them, and we may not even understand them. But wherever we go, we all live by the rules of life for that situation.

God has a set of life rules too. And when you became a Christian, you began a process of adopting God's life rules in place of the others you may have learned in life.

There's just one problem. Instinctively, Christians tend to focus on the rules for interacting with God and downplay the ones for dealing with other people. We assume that until we get a handle on our relationship with God, everything else can wait. But God places a higher priority on how we treat each other than we may think. In fact, God says our ability to relate with other people has a direct impact on our ability to relate to Him. I look forward to the next several weeks together as we explore the dynamics of the different relationships in life and God's life rules for each one.

Session 1

Rules of Engagement

Perhaps the most profound experience of becoming a Christian is the discovery of a brand-new relationship with the God of the universe. Suddenly, the priority of every other relationship gets shuffled as the notion of having a personal heavenly Father begins to sink in. The power and influence that once belonged to people in your life is instantly acknowledged to be God's instead. Your human relationships automatically move down a notch to make way for God at the top.

Everything about this paradigm shift seems to suggest that this new relationship with God is now the most important thing in the world. All other relationships can seem trivial, subservient, and insignificant. In our zeal, we may even conclude that the other relationships don't really matter anymore. As long as things are right with God, all is right.

But God doesn't quite see it that way. In fact, He seems to place surprising emphasis on the health and maturity of our relationships at home, at work, and in our community. And, as we'll see in this first session of *Life Rules*, the success of our relationship with God is actually determined by the success of our relationships with the people around us.

EXERCISE

A Personal Endorsement

It's rare that someone forms his impression of you without the influence of another person helping to paint the picture one way or the other. What people say about you can be a reflection of who you are. That's because personal endorsements offer valuable evidence into our true character. What kind of endorsement would each of the following give you?

- Spouse/Family:
- Coworkers/Clients:
- Friends/Neighbors:
- Adversaries:

What do these reports say about the health and maturity of your relationship with God?

VIDEO NOTES

From the video message, fill in the blanks:

1. Your relationship with God is determined by your relationship with the ________________ God puts in your life.

2. It would be a lot easier to have a religion that focuses on ____GOD____ and leaves everybody else out.

3. As you begin to understand the degree to which your heavenly Father has ____Forgiven____ you, you will realize you've lost your right not to forgive others.

> *"Any fool can make a rule."*
> *—Henry David Thoreau*

NOTES

Bare w/ UNBAREable ppl

-Tracy Safeflight. college trip
-Dawn safe trip boston.
-Carolyn S. carolina.
-Kristin- pray for stress @ work & to Rise above it.
- Joelyn pray for patience w/ scn
• jimmy - pray for job
Pray for Emma She turns 6.

DISCUSSION QUESTIONS

Take a few moments to discuss your answers to these questions with the group.

1. What were some of the unspoken rules for relationships in your family growing up?

2. How do those rules compare to the ones that govern everyday life in the world today?

3. Which is easier, observing "religious" rules or keeping God's rules for loving the other people in our lives? Why?

4. What are some words that describe how God has dealt with you throughout your life?

5. Why would God want us to use His standard when we deal with others?

MILEPOSTS

- The health and maturity of your relationship with God depends on your relationships with other people.
- As God's ambassadors in this world, we are to convey love to those around us.
- When we remember God's love for us, our only response is to love others.

WHAT WILL YOU DO?

As the body of Christ, we need to be accurate reflections of God to the people around us. That's why God places such a high priority on the health of our human relationships. As a Christian, you help to shape people's impression of Christ. Can you list any relationships in which you may not always have represented Christ accurately? Describe.

THINK ABOUT IT

For those relationships listed, are there any steps you could take to begin correcting some misrepresentations? What can you do to prevent future ones?

CHANGING YOUR MIND

God's perspective, found in His Word, reminds us of the priorities of our relationships. Renew your mind by meditating on God's perspective. You can begin by writing down the Scripture below and carrying God's Word with you throughout the day. There's one passage for each week.

"By this all men will know that you are my disciples,
if you love one another."

JOHN 13:35

LAST WEEK...
We saw that we live by a set of rules for every relationship. However, it's not possible to use one set of rules for the people around us and another when we approach God. As God's ambassadors, we are to treat others with the love and respect due them—just as we would with God.

Session 2

Free to Forgive

Following God's rules for life sounds like a great idea, but sometimes it's not easy. It's hard to treat people with love and respect on a regular basis. Especially when they don't deserve it. When we've been mistreated, it may feel more appropriate to punish, ignore, or just avoid the other person.

Perhaps you've been hurt, cheated, or victimized by someone in your life. Surely you aren't expected just to treat that person with love and ignore what they did, are you? At the very least they owe you an apology first, right? Sure, you'd love to be free from the burden of anger, but how do you reconcile God's idealistic standards with the cold, harsh realities you've experienced?

At the heart of forgiveness is a concept that brings a whole new perspective to the pain of your past. In this session, we'll discover three simple steps to finding the freedom of forgiveness in any situation. And in the process, you'll see how God's life rules are not about forgiving and forgetting, but about deciding and remembering.

A Full Acquittal

Have you ever been forgiven? Describe a time when you deserved to have the book thrown at you, but someone let you off scot-free instead.

EXERCISE

VIDEO NOTES

From the video message, fill in the blanks:

1. Forgiveness is a ________________ that we make.
2. Forgiveness is making the decision that someone doesn't ________________ you anymore.
3. Forgiveness doesn't make any sense unless you are a ________________ person.

FORGIVENESS:

4. ________________who you are angry with.
5. ________________what they owe you.
6. ________________to cancel the debt.

> *"Forgiveness is the fragrance the violet sheds on the heel that has crushed it."*
> *—Mark Twain*

NOTES

DISCUSSION QUESTIONS

Take a few moments to discuss your answers to these questions with the group.

1. Why is it so hard to get rid of anger?
2. Why is it so important?
3. Have you ever seen anyone self-destruct because of anger? Describe.
4. Who are some of the people who owe you because they have "stolen" something from you? Explain.
5. Does anger have any "hooks" in you today?
6. What steps would you have to take to rid yourself of ALL anger, as Paul described?

MILEPOSTS

- Forgiveness is a decision that we make.
- Forgiveness is making the decision that someone doesn't owe you anymore.
- Forgiveness doesn't make any sense unless you are a forgiven person.

WHAT WILL YOU DO?

This week, start a list of things that have been taken from you. For each person with whom you are tempted to hold a grudge, define exactly what they owe you.

THINK ABOUT IT

What did you owe God as a result of your sin? Why? How does God's forgiveness impact your ability to forgive others?

CHANGING YOUR MIND

Meditate on this verse throughout the week as a reminder that you are free to forgive because you are forgiven.

"Be kind and compassionate to one another,
forgiving each other, just as in Christ God forgave you."

EPHESIANS 4:32

LAST WEEK...
We learned that forgiveness is possible even in the most inconceivable situations. That means even the deepest bitterness can't keep you from pursuing God's rules for the relationships in your life. Forgiveness begins with a clear definition of what is owed you and it ends with a decision to cancel the debt.

Session 3

The Act of Acceptance

Of all the rules that describe our attitudes and actions toward others, *Accept* may be the toughest to grasp. We know what it looks like to forgive someone—to let them off the hook, or out of the doghouse. But exactly what does it mean to accept someone?

Acceptance is commonly viewed as the absence of rejection. If you don't have anything against someone, then they're basically accepted, right? Your position is neutral. But from God's perspective, that's not exactly what it's all about.

As we're about to see, acceptance goes beyond merely holding a neutral position toward someone. In fact, true acceptance requires that we become proactive in our effort to accept others. In this session, we'll see how acceptance is one of the most influential forces in the world. It decides our emotions and shapes the course of our lives. In Jesus' life, acceptance was the foundation of a ministry that portrayed the essence of God to the world. And in our lives it's not just a good suggestion, it's a life rule.

EXERCISE

Degrees of Acceptance

Which of the following would evoke the greatest sense of acceptance for you? Rank them in order:

a. Your in-laws write a letter to express their admiration for you.
b. Your boss gives you recognition in front of the whole company.
c. Your parents verbalize how proud they are of you.
d. Your classmates vote you Most Popular.
e. Your neighbors throw a surprise party for your birthday.

Why do some things make us feel more accepted than others? Explain.

VIDEO NOTES

From the video message, fill in the blanks:

1. Your life has been shaped by doses of ________________ and acceptance.
2. We are far more open to the ________________ of people who accept us than people who lecture us.
3. God says we are to accept people before they are ________________.
4. Jesus did not come into this world to be ________________.

> *"Our grandchildren accept us for ourselves, without rebuke or effort to change us, as no one in our entire lives has ever done...."*
> —Ruth Goode

NOTES

DISCUSSION QUESTIONS

Take a few moments to discuss your answers to these questions with the group.

1. Around what person or group of people do you feel the least accepted? Why?

2. How is God's standard for acceptance different from the world's standard?

3. Why should we accept each other just as God accepted us?

4. What person is the most difficult for you to accept? Why?

5. What gesture of acceptance could you make toward that person this week?

MILEPOSTS

- Your life has been shaped by doses of rejection and acceptance.
- We are far more open to the influence of people who accept us than people who lecture us.
- God says we are to accept people before they are acceptable.
- Jesus did not come into this world to be right.

WHAT WILL YOU DO?

When we struggle to be accepting, it's because we hold standards that are not attainable by the other person. It will be easier to be accepting when you've identified the false standards that cause you to reject others. In the space below, identify someone you struggle to accept. Beside it, describe the standard you are embracing that causes you to reject that person.

THINK ABOUT IT

God wants us to abandon our false standards and adopt His standards for dealing with the people in our lives. For each of the false standards you listed, briefly describe God's standard that should be upheld instead.

What words or actions could you take to demonstrate God's standards this week?

CHANGING YOUR MIND

False standards of acceptance can be difficult to replace. Train your mind to God's standard of acceptance by meditating on this verse throughout the week.

"Accept one another, then, just as Christ accepted you, in order to bring praise to God."

ROMANS 15:7

LAST WEEK...
We learned that acceptance is not simply a neutral posture, but a spiritual act of receiving and affirming someone else. Many of our standards for accepting people are false or arbitrary. But when it comes to accepting others, God wants us to use the same standard He uses for accepting us—we are accepted without being proven acceptable.

Session 4

It's Your Serve

Serve. Just the thought of it can evoke images of toil, drudgery, and obligation. Most people don't mind giving back a little now and then. But adopting a lifestyle of service can be a bit of a stretch. Motivation can be fleeting. Especially when you consider that some of the people in our lives deserve the opposite of service from us.

But there's a surprising dynamic to serving that we often miss. It's not simply a matter of performing labor or meeting a need. The greatest benefit of serving goes to the one who serves. That's because the act of serving triggers a shift in personal perspective that impacts a person's whole outlook on life. And there's no other way to replicate it.

In this session, we'll explore the secret opportunity that exists when you serve without obligation. We'll also examine the unique way serving affects relationships and leads to personal breakthroughs that can't be accomplished by any other means. And we'll see why it's the key to freedom for the person who serves.

Who's Serving Who?

Has anyone ever served you? How did that make you feel toward that person? Briefly describe a time when you were served.

Is someone more influential because they serve others? Explain.

VIDEO NOTES

From the video message, fill in the blanks:

To serve means:

1. When you see a need, ________________ it; when something needs to be done, ________________ it.
2. If you continue to serve only yourself, eventually you will be all ________________ yourself.
3. When we decide to serve, we break the ________________ of self-centeredness.

> *"I have found the paradox that if I love until it hurts, then there is no hurt, but only more love."*
> *—Mother Teresa*

NOTES

DISCUSSION QUESTIONS

Take a few moments to discuss your answers to these questions with the group.

1. What is the most inspiring example of service you've ever heard about?

2. Why is it counterintuitive to serve others?

3. What gives God the right to command us to serve the people who have hurt us?

4. Name someone in your life who is in need of being served.

5. Name one way you will serve that person this week.

MILEPOSTS

- To serve means: When you see a need, meet it; when something needs to be done, do it.

- If you continue to serve only yourself, eventually you will be all by yourself.

- When we decide to serve, we break the control of self-centeredness.

WHAT WILL YOU DO?

We are called to serve whenever we see a need or see something that needs to be done. Where are you most likely to find yourself called to serve this week? What action can you take to respond in service?

THINK ABOUT IT

Aside from building a bridge relationally, the greatest benefit of serving is that it helps us break free from selfish desires. Name at least one benefit that you would experience by following through on the action(s) you named in the previous exercise.

CHANGING YOUR MIND

Meditate on this verse to remind you of the value of serving as a way to exercise your freedom from the sinful nature.

"You, my brothers, were called to be free.
But do not use your freedom to indulge the sinful nature;
rather, serve one another in love."

GALATIANS 5:13

LAST WEEK...
We saw that there's more to serving than simply meeting someone else's needs. Serving represents one of the most profound opportunities to impact our relationships. Most of all, serving brings an even greater benefit to the one who serves, by creating freedom from our sinful, self-serving nature.

Session 5

The Courage to Encourage

Perhaps you already consider yourself to be an encourager to those around you. Maybe it's your habit to speak a kind word or to lend moral support to someone in need. You enjoy being a source of motivation for others. You've got the encouragement rule covered.

Well, this session could cause you to rethink all that. Because, as we're about to discover, to encourage means more than giving a pep talk to inspire your fellow Christians. In fact, if you do it right, there might not be much uplifting about it at all.

In this session, we'll see how the word *encouragement* as used in the Bible is much more invasive than a friendly affirmation. As the apostle Paul explains, there's a snare that can deceive and overtake any of us without warning. And our only hope is that one of our Christian brothers will see it developing and come to our aid before it's too late. Encouragement is God's tool for such a rescue mission. And it should be a life rule for every Christian.

EXERCISE

Be Encouraged

Which of the following would you consider to be the most encouraging thing that could happen? Rank them in order.

a. Your spouse says, "I love you."
b. Your boss tells you you're doing a great job.
c. A friend cautions you not to become lazy or give up.
d. An acquaintance unexpectedly asks if you are involved in impropriety.

VIDEO NOTES

From the video message, fill in the blanks:

1. God has called us to mind one another's

   ________________ .

2. We quit behaving before we quit ________________ .

3. To encourage means to appeal, to beg, to urge, to

   ________________ .

> *"'Tis a great confidence in a friend to tell him your faults; greater to tell him his."*
> *—Benjamin Franklin*

NOTES

DISCUSSION QUESTIONS

Take a few moments to discuss your answers to these questions with the group.

1. Why is it so awkward to approach someone directly when they need intervention?

2. How do you think you would respond if someone poked his nose into your business?

3. Why are Christians commanded to get involved in each other's lives?

4. Who comes to mind as someone who has started down a path that begs your intervention?

5. How will you fulfill your Christian responsibility to them this week?

6. Who, in your life, feels empowered to speak up if you should start to drift?

MILEPOSTS

- God has called us to mind one another's business.
- We quit behaving before we quit believing.
- To encourage means to appeal, to beg, to urge, to exhort.

WHAT WILL YOU DO?

During this session, did anyone in particular come to mind? Have you been talking *about* someone instead of talking *to* him or her? Have you been *praying* instead of *saying*? This week, consider whether God might use you to be a friend to that person. It might not be as awkward as you think. Your approach can be appealing if you are honest, humble, and present yourself as a genuine friend. Asking, "Is everything okay?" or, "Would you mind sharing your situation with me?" might be all it takes to establish true rapport. In the space below, brainstorm some conversation points that would help you communicate with this person in an appealing way.

THINK ABOUT IT

What would happen if you fell under the deceitfulness of sin? Would the Christians around you take the initiative to speak up? In the space below, identify one or two people you trust. Then invite them to make you aware of blind spots now and in the future.

CHANGING YOUR MIND

When it comes to this issue, sometimes it's uncomfortable to be bold. Meditate on this verse this week as an encouragement to yourself that you need to be an encouragement to others.

"But encourage one another daily,
as long as it is called Today,
so that none of you may be hardened by sin's deceitfulness."

HEBREWS 3:13

LAST WEEK...
We saw that there's a lot more to encouragement than our English word suggests. The original Greek word reveals that the apostle Paul intends for us to mind each other's business when it comes to sin. Encouragement may seem awkward, but it's one of the most important services each member of Christ's body performs.

Session 6

I Submit

The word *submit* is inherently controversial. It seems to conjure up a variety of mental images. Understandably, many of us are uncomfortable with the idea of submitting to certain people. What if they aren't trustworthy? What if they take advantage of us?

But in this context, submitting doesn't mean doing whatever the other person tells you to do. And despite our stigmas with the concept, submitting to one another is a crucial life rule for Christians. In fact, when we truly understand the meaning of submitting, it becomes one of the most important influences within a Christian community.

In this session, we'll examine what God really means when He instructs us to submit to one another. We'll also reveal one of the most common motives for submitting—and why it often leads to disappointment. And finally, we'll study the ultimate example of submission: when Christ put our needs ahead of His own.

Word Association

What do you think of when you hear the word *submit?* In the space below, describe the mental image that this word conjures for you. Share your answers with the group.

EXERCISE

VIDEO NOTES

From the video message, fill in the blanks:

1. Paul asks us to submit to one another because it shows reverence and respect for ________________ .
2. Submit means to consider ________________ better than ourselves.
3. When He was on this earth, Jesus never pulled ________________ .
4. Jesus ________________ His power for others.

"Politeness is to human nature what warmth is to wax."
—Arthur Schopenhauer

NOTES

DISCUSSION QUESTIONS

Take a few moments to discuss your answers to these questions with the group.

1. What's the difference between submitting to someone in authority and submitting to one another?

2. Why is it counterintuitive to submit to each other?

3. How might the world be different if Christians submitted to one another?

4. How is this command different from the way you interact with people currently?

5. Who comes to mind as someone you should submit yourself to the way Christ submitted Himself for you?

6. What is one step you could take this week to submit yourself to that person?

MILEPOSTS

- Our motive for submitting to one another is to show reverence and respect for Christ.
- Submit means to consider others better than ourselves.
- When He was on this earth, Jesus never pulled rank.
- Instead, Jesus leveraged His power for others.

WHAT WILL YOU DO?

Perhaps we hesitate to submit because it just doesn't seem to work. We've tried putting others first, but they just ran all over us even more. We've tried being submissive, but we just seem to get further and further behind. As we've just seen, our reason for submitting should not be because it "works," but because it shows reverence for Christ. In order to help you expose your flawed motives, list several situations in which you feel called to submit. Beside each one, briefly describe any erroneous expectations you might be tempted to entertain.

Example: Submit to coworker so that he will see my example, change his ways, and we will finally get along better.

THINK ABOUT IT

How does it express reverence for Christ when we submit to one another? For each of the situations mentioned in the previous exercise, briefly describe how your actions would honor Christ, regardless of the response of those around you.

CHANGING YOUR MIND

Meditating on Scripture is the best way to align our hearts with God's desires. Carry this passage of Scripture with you this week as a reminder of our core motivation for submitting to one another.

"Submit to one another out of reverence for Christ."

EPHESIANS 5:21

LEADER'S GUIDE

So, You're the Leader...

Is that intimidating? Perhaps exciting? No doubt you have some mental pictures of what it will look like, what you will say, and how it will go. Before you get too far into the planning process, there are some things you should know about leading a small-group discussion. We've compiled some tried and true techniques here to help you.

BASICS ABOUT LEADING

1. **Don't teach...facilitate**—Perhaps you've been in a Sunday school class or Bible study in which the leader could answer any question and always had something interesting to say. It's easy to think you need to be like that too. Relax. You don't. Leading a small group is quite different. Instead of being the featured act at the party, think of yourself as the host or hostess behind the scenes. Your primary job is to create an environment where people feel comfortable and to keep the meeting generally on track. Your party is most successful when your guests do most of the talking.

2. **Cultivate discussion**—It's also easy to think that the meeting lives or dies by *your* ideas. In reality, what makes a small-group meeting successful are the ideas of everyone in the group. The most valuable thing you can do is to get people to share their thoughts. That's how the

relationships in your group will grow and thrive. Here's a rule: The impact of your study material will typically never exceed the impact of the relationships through which it was studied. The more meaningful the relationships, the more meaningful the study. In a sterile environment, even the best material is suppressed.

3. **Point to the material**—A good host or hostess gets the party going by offering delectable hors d'oeuvres and beverages. You too should be ready to serve up "delicacies" from the material. Sometimes you will simply read the discussion questions and invite everyone to respond. At other times, you may encourage someone to share their own ideas. Remember, some of the best treats are the ones your guests will bring to the party. Go with the flow of the meeting, and be ready to pop out of the kitchen as needed.

4. **Depart from the material**—A talented ministry team has carefully designed this study for your small group. But that doesn't mean you should follow every part word for word. Knowing how and when to depart from the material is a valuable art. Nobody knows more about your people than you do. The narratives, questions, and exercises are here to provide a framework for discovery.

However, every group is motivated differently. Sometimes, the best way to start a small-group discussion is simply to ask, "Does anyone have any personal insights or revelations they'd like to share from this week's material?" Then sit back and listen.

5. **Stay on track**—Conversation is like the currency of a small-group discussion. The more interchange, the healthier the "economy." However, you need to keep your objectives in mind. If your goal is to have a meaningful experience with this material, then you should make sure the discussion is contributing to that end. It's easy to get off on a tangent. Be prepared to interject politely and refocus the group. You may need to say something like, "Excuse me, we're obviously all interested in this subject; however, I just want to make sure we cover all the material for this week."

6. **Above all, pray**—The best communicators are the ones who manage to get out of God's way enough to let Him communicate *through* them. That's important to keep in mind. Books don't teach God's Word; neither do sermons or group discussions. God Himself speaks into the hearts of men and women, and prayer is our vital channel to

communicate directly with Him. Cover your efforts in prayer. You don't just want God present at your meeting, you want Him to direct it.

We hope you find these suggestions helpful. And we hope you enjoy leading this study. You will find additional guides and suggestions for each session in the Leader's Guide notes that follow.

Leader's Guide Session Notes

SESSION 1—RULES OF ENGAGEMENT

KEY POINT

In every situation in life there are unwritten, unspoken rules that govern how we treat each other. Often, Christians downplay the importance of how they treat each other, thinking that how they treat God is much more important. But God doesn't see it that way. Our attitudes toward each other are a direct reflection of our attitude toward Him, because He has commanded us to love and respect each other. Therefore, the success of our relationship with God is impacted by the success of our relationships with the people in our lives.

EXERCISE—A PERSONAL ENDORSEMENT

The purpose of this exercise is to suggest that what people say about us is an indication of our character. We can measure how we are doing with God by our character; and we can begin to measure our character by the report others give about us.

Video Notes

1. Your relationship with God is determined by your relationship with the people God puts in your life.

2. It would be a lot easier to have a religion that focuses on God and leaves everybody else out.

3. As you begin to understand the degree to which your heavenly Father has forgiven you, you will realize you've lost your right not to forgive others.

Notes for Discussion Questions:

1. What were some of the unspoken rules for relationships in your family growing up?

   The purpose of this opening question is to get people comfortable talking and sharing ideas in the group. One of the best ways to do that is to ask them to talk about themselves. Encourage each person to describe at least one thing about the relationships he or she experienced growing up.

2. How do those rules compare to the ones that govern everyday life in the world today?
   The purpose of this question is to transition from the past to the present. This will set the stage for comparing the rules of the world around us with the life rules of God's Word.

3. Which is easier, observing "religious" rules or keeping God's rules for loving the other people in our lives? Why?
   Relationships can be complicated. Sometimes it would be easier to go through the motions with God than to truly sort out the complexities with another person. God wants us to see that He's not interested in our "religion," but in seeing us take the time to implement His life rules in all of our relationships.

4. What are some words that describe how God has dealt with you throughout your life?

   In dealing with us, God has set the example of how we are to deal with others. Love is the standard. Anything less is not enough.

5. Why would God want us to use His standard when we deal with others?

   God's agenda for all Christians is to gradually conform them into the likeness of Christ. Our relationships with each other provide a vital training ground for that process.

What Will You Do?

This exercise will help participants take a careful look at the relationships around them. They should be able to identify any broken relationships in which they have not been modeling God's life rules.

Think About It

Now participants should identify specific ways they can respond to the message of this session. If certain relationships came to mind, now is the time to take the first step to begin implementing God's life rules in those situations.

SESSION 2—FREE TO FORGIVE

KEY POINT

Forgiveness is an essential foundation for all the other life rules. Unless you can forgive, it will be impossible to abide by the other life rules with consistency. Forgiveness is not so much for the one who receives it, but for the one who gives it. It is the key to freedom from the pain of the past. Forgiveness doesn't make any sense...except to forgiven people.

EXERCISE—A FULL ACQUITTAL

Earthly examples of forgiveness are tangible parallels of God's forgiveness toward us. The purpose here is to remind participants that they have been forgiven, and therefore it is appropriate for them to forgive.

VIDEO NOTES

1. Forgiveness is a decision that we make.
2. Forgiveness is making the decision that someone doesn't owe you anymore.

3. Forgiveness doesn't make any sense unless you are a forgiven person.

FORGIVENESS:

4. Identify who you are angry with.
5. Determine what they owe you.
6. Decide to cancel the debt.

Notes for Discussion Questions

1. Why is it so hard to get rid of anger?

   This is a general question to get participants thinking about the dynamics of anger. There are several useful conclusions they may draw, including: anger should be avoided at the start; anger feels like something has been taken; anger suggests that justice must be rendered.

2. Why is it so important?

   Anger that is not removed can control us. We must get rid of anger to ensure that our lives are completely free from its unhealthy influence—we should be under the control of God instead.

3. Have you ever seen anyone self-destruct because of anger? Describe.

   As this question suggests, anger causes destruction from the inside. This question will likely elicit true-life, interesting examples of this principle from members of the group.

4. Who are some of the people who owe you because they have "stolen" something from you? Explain.

   This question draws participants into the process of eradicating anger. The first step in this process is to identify the people we are angry with.

5. Does anger have any "hooks" in you today?

   If we're honest, most of us can identify those we are tempted to be angry with. This self-examination question is an opportunity to determine whether anger is a serious threat or not.

6. What steps would you have to take to rid yourself of ALL anger, as Paul described?

   The steps to eradicating anger were outlined in the video message for this session. Getting rid of ALL anger requires an ongoing practice of identifying whenever someone "takes" something and choosing to cancel the debt.

What Will You Do?

This exercise builds on the suggestion mentioned during the video message for this session. Identifying what was taken is a crucial part of defining an offense and canceling the debt. For maximum results, this exercise should become a part of our lifestyle.

Think About It

Take some time as a group to fully embrace what it means to be forgiven. God's forgiveness of us is significant. Therefore our forgiveness toward others should be significant as well.

SESSION 3—THE ACT OF ACCEPTANCE

KEY POINT

Accepting goes beyond merely holding a neutral position toward someone. It means receiving someone to ourselves. Christ receives us to Himself, and that is the model we are to follow when interacting with others. Accepting is a proactive effort of making sure the people around us feel accepted. Acceptance is a basic human need; when someone senses our acceptance, it draws them to us, enabling us to influence them with God's love.

EXERCISE—DEGREES OF ACCEPTANCE

There are various factors that determine how deeply we feel acceptance. While the acceptance of peers is powerful, most people tend to feel an even greater need to be accepted in the closest relationships in life, such as family.

Video Notes

1. Your life has been shaped by doses of rejection and acceptance.
2. We are far more open to the influence of people who accept us than people who lecture us.
3. God says we are to accept people before they are acceptable.
4. Jesus did not come into this world to be right.

Notes for Discussion Questions

1. Around what person or group of people do you feel the least accepted? Why?

   The main purpose of this question is to cause participants to rehearse what it feels like not to be accepted. This will motivate us to make others feel accepted.

2. How is God's standard for acceptance different from the world's standard?

   This question should bring out how the world tends to grant conditional acceptance—based on merit and performance. God's standard is unconditional.

3. Why should we accept each other just as God accepted us?

   Having been accepted by God, it is only appropriate that we extend the same measure of acceptance to others. (See Matthew 18:23–35.)

4. What person is the most difficult for you to accept? Why?

   This is a point of application, prompting participants to identify someone they can practice accepting unconditionally.

5. What gesture of acceptance could you make toward that person this week?

   Encourage participants to identify some tangible act they will carry out this week. You may choose to follow up next week to see how they did.

What Will You Do?

It can be very helpful to identify the specific, erroneous standards we expect others to meet. When we isolate these unspoken expectations, we will likely see how unfair and inappropriate it is for Christians to make such demands of others.

Think About It

In similar fashion, it can be very helpful to articulate God's standards. This exercise can be very helpful, giving participants a clear point of reference for the standards they are to use with other people.

SESSION 4—IT'S YOUR SERVE

KEY POINT

The call to serve is not simply a functional mandate to make sure certain tasks get done. It is an invitation to leverage a very powerful principle. Serving others when there is no obligation to do so is an opportunity to impact relationships in the most profound way. In addition, serving is one of the best ways we can break the bond of self-centeredness in our own lives.

EXERCISE—WHO'S SERVING WHO?

When we serve others, it actually serves us too. First, it gives us influence with the people we serve. Second, it tends to enhance our relationships overall. And finally, it frees us from the destructive tendencies of selfishness.

VIDEO NOTES

1. When you see a need, <u>meet</u> it; when something needs to be done, <u>do</u> it.

2. If you continue to serve only yourself, eventually you will be all by yourself.
3. When we decide to serve, we break the control of self-centeredness.

Notes for Discussion Questions

1. What is the most inspiring example of service you've ever heard about?

   The purpose of this question is to help the group define what service means. Once participants have shared several ideas, everyone should clearly understand what the term means.

2. Why is it counterintuitive to serve others?

   Serving others when there is no obligation to do so does not make sense in the world's economy. Like many other principles of God, serving is tied to a spiritual economy. Growing in Christ is a process of learning to trust that the spiritual economy supercedes the world's economy.

3. What gives God the right to command us to serve the people who have hurt us?

   The foundation of God's command to serve is the issue of ownership—as willing recipients of God's service to us, we now belong to Him.

4. Name someone in your life who is in need of being served.

   This question turns the conversation toward application. Encourage everyone in the group to identify someone to serve, regardless of whether they deserve it or not.

5. Name one way you will serve that person this week.

   Likewise, encourage everyone to name a specific way they can apply what they've learned this week. You may choose to follow up next week to see how everyone did.

What Will You Do?

This exercise prompts participants to be on the lookout for opportunities that can pop up in everyday situations. The goal is to develop an ongoing attitude of anticipating potential chances to serve.

Think About It

If participants really apply the previous exercise, there will be many benefits. This exercise helps them rehearse one more time what those can be. They may include improved relationships and even an improved perspective on life.

SESSION 5—THE COURAGE TO ENCOURAGE

Key Point

Most people have a rather benign mental picture of the word *encourage.* But in Scripture the call to encourage is actually quite invasive. It requires the courage to step forward and address uncomfortable situations. It can be awkward. You can face rejection. But it is one of the most important responsibilities within the body of Christ. We are called to encourage in order to keep our brothers and sisters from falling into the deceitfulness of sin.

Exercise—Be Encouraged

At first glance, compliments may seem like the best encouragements. Ironically, however, most scriptural examples of encouragement might not feel very encouraging at all. Encouragement is not about making someone feel good about himself; it's about helping someone stay on track with God.

Video Notes

1. God has called us to mind one another's business.
2. We quit behaving before we quit believing.
3. To encourage means to appeal, to beg, to urge, to exhort.

Notes for Discussion Questions

1. Why is it so awkward to approach someone directly when they need intervention?
   Without a doubt, confrontation can be awkward. The main objective of this question is for participants to recognize that it's not easy... and that's okay.

2. How do you think you would respond if someone poked his nose into your business?
   You can expect to feel uncomfortable as well. And once again... it's okay. God does not always call us to do things that feel right. But that doesn't mean they aren't important.

3. Why are Christians commanded to get involved in each other's lives?

   Scripture refers to Christians together as a body. It is God's design that we thrive only when we interact properly with each other. We were created to need each other; sometimes that is the only way to grow in Christ and guard against sin.

4. Who comes to mind as someone who has started down a path that begs your intervention?

   Moving toward application, this question prompts participants to consider whether they should take action to help someone around them.

5. How will you fulfill your Christian responsibility to them this week?

   Following suit, participants should envision what practical steps should be taken to provide intervention that will help those who need it.

6. Who, in your life, feels empowered to speak up if you should start to drift?

   On a similar note, we can take steps to make sure we are as approachable as possible by our fellow believers. It is wise to invite others to watch out for us, empowering them to intervene as they see necessary.

What Will You Do?

This exercise goes a step further, helping participants to identify specific talking points for approaching someone who needs encouragement. The main benefit of planning this out is to minimize awkwardness and make the conversation productive and effective.

Think About It

As a follow-up to the discussion questions, this exercise will prompt participants to enlist one or two fellow believers to come to their aid in the future if he or she ever drifts. You may suggest that group members form a buddy system to accomplish this.

SESSION 6—I SUBMIT

Key Point

Many people think the biblical concept of submitting means allowing someone to trample all over you. But the life rule of submitting to one another means to act as if others are more important than ourselves. If everyone practiced this, God's grace would be demonstrated in His people in unmistakable ways.

Exercise—Word Association

This exercise is intended to expose any inaccurate preconceptions about the term *submit.* It's important to eliminate these slanted views so that everyone gains a full and proper understanding of God's command to submit to one another.

Video Notes

1. Paul asks us to submit to one another because it shows reverence and respect for Jesus Christ.

2. Submit means to consider <u>others</u> better than ourselves.
3. When He was on this earth, Jesus never pulled <u>rank</u>.
4. Jesus <u>leveraged</u> His power for others.

Notes for Discussion Questions

1. What's the difference between submitting to someone in authority and submitting to one another?
   It's important for everyone in the group to understand that we are not talking about the principle of authority in this session. When we submit to each other, it is not because we are under each other's authority, but because we choose to honor each other in the name of Christ.

2. Why is it counterintuitive to submit to each other?
   Submitting is counterintuitive only from the world's point of view. This question simply acknowledges that it may seem strange to always defer to others, but from God's perspective, it makes perfect sense.

3. How might the world be different if Christians submitted to one another?

   There are no right or wrong answers to this question. The discussion should reveal that submitting has a positive effect among Christians and on their witness to the world.

4. How is this command different from the way you interact with people currently?

   This question prompts participants to examine whether they personally demonstrate submission. Encourage the people in your group to share honestly about themselves.

5. Who comes to mind as someone you should submit yourself to the way Christ submitted Himself for you?

   In order to put this life rule into practice, we need to envision real situations where it can be applied. In response to this question, participants can make a variety of suggestions to each other.

6. What is one step you could take this week to submit yourself to that person?

   In the same way, this question helps participants envision what submission might look like in their own lives. Make sure the people in your group leave with a clear understanding of the concept.

What Will You Do?

In response to this exercise, participants should be able to list several common false expectations. The main point is that our motive for submitting must not be because it "works." That will inevitably lead to disappointment.

Think About It

Our motive for submitting is to show reverence for Christ—an objective that we can accomplish regardless of how the situation turns out. This exercise helps participants establish the right expectations and to realize the positive benefits of showing reverence for Christ.

Taking Care of Business

Finding God At Work

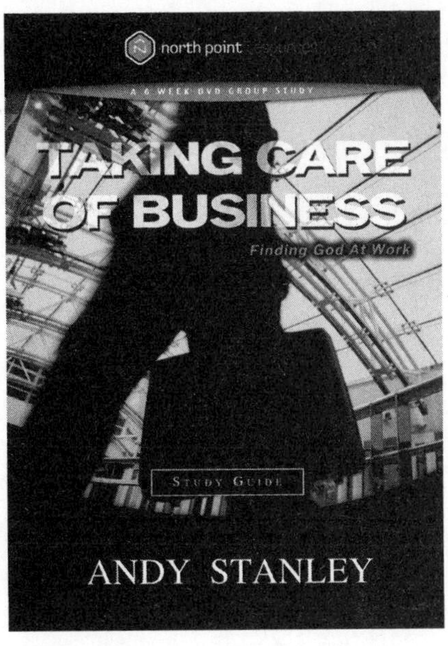

God created work and intends for us to make the most of it! Gain His perspective and get equipped to make changes that allow you to thrive in the workplace.

Study Guide 978-1-59052-491-3
DVD 978-1-59052-492-6

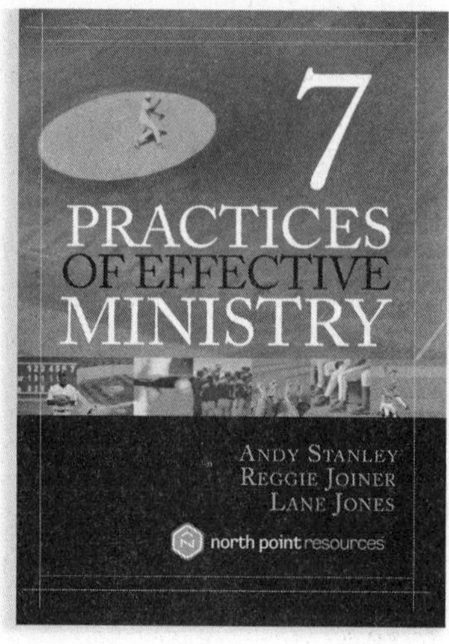

7 Practices of Effective Ministry
Andy Stanley, Lane Jones, Reggie Joiner

An insightful and entertaining parable for every ministry leader who yearns for a more simplified approach to ministry.

ISBN: 978-1-59052-373-3
$19.99 Hardback
Church Resources

Creating Community
Andy Stanley and Bill Willits

Creating Community delivers a successful template for building and nurturing small groups in your church. Andy Stanley and Bill Willits reveal the formula developed over ten years at North Point Community Church for one of the most successful and admired small group ministries in the country.

ISBN: 978-1-59052-396-4
$19.99 Hardback
Church Resources

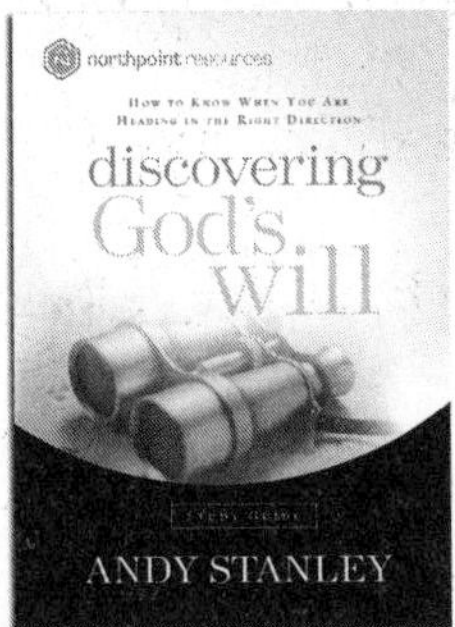

Discovering God's Will Study Guide & DVD

Andy Stanley

God has a personal vision for your life and He wants you to know it even more than you do. Determining God's will can be a difficult process, especially when we need to make a decision in a hurry. In this eight part series, Andy Stanley discusses God's providential, moral, and personal will and how He uses other people and the principles of Scripture to guide us.

Study Guide 978-1-59052-379-7, $9.99
DVD 978-1-59052-380-3, $24.99

Parental Guidance Study Guide & DVD

Andy Stanley and Reggie Joiner

Our lives are influenced by our relationships, experiences, and decisions. Therefore our priority as parents should be to enhance our child's relationship with us, advance our child's relationship with God, and influence our child's relationship with those outside the home.

Study Guide 978-1-59052-381-0, $9.99
DVD 978-1-59052-378-0, $24.99

Defining Moments Study Guide & DVD

Andy Stanley

It is no secret that what you don't know CAN hurt you. In spite of that, we still go out of our way at times to avoid the truth. Learn how to discern the truth and apply those "defining moments" in your life with this DVD and study guide.

Study Guide 978-1-59052-464-0, $9.99
DVD 978-1-59052-465-7, $24.99

The Best Question Ever Study Guide & DVD

Andy Stanley

Can you think of a question that has the potential to foolproof your relationships, your marriage, your finances, even your health? A question that, had you asked it and followed its leading, would have enabled you to avoid your greatest regret? Read *The Best Question Ever Study Guide* to find out how to foolproof your life.

Study Guide 978-1-59052-462-6, $9.99
DVD 978-1-59052-463-3, $24.99